MW00943241

PICK YOUR
POISON

Poetry by Denise Walker

Other titles by Denise Walker

Cedar Valley Novel

PICK YOUR
POISON

Poetry by Denise Walker

Cover design by Lydia Stewart

For my tribe

Forward

These poems are not in any particular order because addiction is not orderly. Recovery is not orderly. It is not sorted into neat chapters or accompanied by an instruction manual. Addiction recovery at its core is unpredictable, chaotic, and at most times, overwhelming. I needed help navigating early sobriety and creating poetry was a healthy way to cope with all the poison leaving my system.

Alcohol. My poison. It was all fun and games until it wasn't. Maybe you know what I'm talking about: summer day drinks with friends, happy hours with coworkers, the beer or three after a miserable day at work, or the celebratory bottle of prosecco on your anniversary. Somehow all the *fun* turned to finding ways to sneak it into music festivals, actively hunting for the best (cheapest/longest) happy hours, a bottle of wine as a daily celebration for a good day at work or a reward for making it through a bad day at work—they became interchangeable. Suddenly you're avoiding people who don't drink, avoiding dry social engagements, bringing two bottles of wine to book club (one to share and one for you), and losing the ability to sleep without a solid mickey* in your system. It gets worse. Alcohol has us by the throat and its grip is getting tighter yet we keep on drinking and we won't stop until it kills us. Unless... what, I am still trying to figure out.

*a mickey is a Canadian term for a small bottle (375mL) of hard alcohol

What was it that convinced me to stop? Was it waking up still drunk most days and having to cancel appointments, commitments, promises with the excuse that I was "sick"? Was it because I was so damn tired of being hungover and shrouded by shame every single day? Was it the unshakable brain fog and constant inability to focus? Was is the crippling guilt that I knew I was killing myself, but kept at it, regardless of the consequences? Yes! All of the above! I wanted to be free! And sobriety gave me exactly what I wanted. At the same time, it taught me that even if you're armed to the teeth and shouldering five backpacks worth of gear, it's impossible to be 100% prepared for what recovery has in store for you.

Recovery is isolating. There are poems here for that.
Recovery is blissful. There are poems here for that.
Recovery is confusing. There are poems here for that.
Recovery is enlightening. There are poems here for that.
Recovery is painful. There are poems here for that.
Recovery is magical. There are poems here for that.
Recovery is terrifying. There are poems here for that.

My poison is alcohol but recovery is not a singular path. There are many things that can poison our lives: trauma (emotional or physical), illness (mental or otherwise), or any addiction under the sun. Anything that steals our truth and our happiness is a poison. The great news is that these poisons have an antidote: recovery. Recovery is beautiful, brutal, truthful, maddening, amazing, and honestly the worst/best rollercoaster we can ever decide to ride. Whatever poison brought you here, you're not on this journey alone. Let these words light your way. Let them inspire you, guide you, anger you, and comfort you.

Let them wake you.

I'M A HUMAN COCKTAIL IN THE PITCH BLACK
BURN, MOLOTOV, BURN

LIKE THE CHANGING OF THE TIDE
THESE FEELINGS TOO WILL FADE

Maze

my mind is a maze without any exits
where the only way (we think) is through
you've never been here, & neither have I
has anyone?

you told me, "you can't trust your own mind
it's going to get harder before it gets worse"
& you were right

every turn, we're back at the start
& the start is darker at every turn
when did we get here?
how did we get so lost?

it's been five labyrinthine years
& all I think now is,
are you even here?
am I?
because you told me,
all those years ago, you told me,
"you can't trust your own mind"

Ache

it's 18:18 & I'm failing
11 times I've agreed to give in
& trying for the 12th time to say no

did I even drive home?
the memories are misty
my mind was...
where was my mind?

my hands ache terribly for the ice
on the other side of the glass
my gums
my god, even my gums
ache

"don't tell anyone!
no, don't tell anyone," you say, frantic
"they'll stop you
you want this
it's okay"

NO I am screaming
literally screaming at
who?
I can't remember
I can't remember
what it's like to have a thought other than this one
I've agreed to give in 14 times now
& said...

where are my walls?
where is my fear?
all I have here,
now,
is desire,
& the only thing left to say is yes

It's Too Late When You Start to Lie

here again
surrounded by the inevitable black
my only defence is to let it in
whisp by whisp
whisper by whisper

you should turn back
this isn't a place for the seasoned
let alone the weak

I sold my soul
but still The Darkness comes
a merchant I can't avoid
paid by others' love that I steal in kind

the line is so blurred, it's barely there
but you can still change your mind
you'll know it's too late
when you start to lie

Pick Your Poison

deep indulgence takes you deeper
to the darkest side of nostalgia
where your skin is pricked with blood lust &
a voraciousness to tear into the gory past
elevated memories
falsities
romanticized in twilight
fear upon fear catastrophically collides with hope
what feels worse
the truth or
the numbness?
what do you want more
the real
or the dream?
caged on this slab
needles pumping in sensation
the veins can't take it
the emotions
the brain won't make it
choose night or nightmare
light or lightning
neither is worth it
& neither will save you
it's time to grit your fangs
& bear it

Brachial Supernova

throw me off the edge of the Earth to land amongst
the starred abyss
let my body explode along with the supernovas
free my cerebrum
release my vertebrae
eject my soul
inject my soul
sucked into the wrist, creeping into the vein
swirl, brilliant black into the crook of your arm
jump, vein to artery
choke off the brachial line
breathe, baby, breathe
invite your heart to soar to exothermic heights
blasting apart
into space & into me

Hug Me

is it possible to be squeezed too tightly?
go on, embrace me until
my cells burst

Band-Aids

I feel everything
it was my choice, but it still rips & shreds my insides
I sent the cure away
& now I see things for what they really are

I see *everything*
the barbed wire & the lies
the fake mentality, the tricks, the cycles
how none of that was the real me
but when it's stripped away, what will be left?

was my laugh real?
were my jokes? am I funny?
I've spent seven days inside of myself, looking out
falling deeper in
what falsities did I weave to stay hidden?
who am I, really?

every part that's torn away,
like Band-Aids made of thorns
is it cleansing me
or leaving me holed & worn?

the fucking worst part is that I can make it stop
I can, in an instant
I crave that mask, that anesthetic
but if I can just bear it a little while longer
I'll be free
I'll be real & happy & able to deal
at least I think that's what they told me…

Bedroom Door

you're always leaving
& that's fine
but every time I stay
the floor falls from beneath my feet
it has nothing to do with you
but, maybe it could

Derailed

tonight I will jump off the cliff
& spend the evening in free fall
I don't want this, of course I don't
but I'm like a runaway train;
something is very wrong with my brakes

I know what it's like on safe ground
it's warm & it's bliss
I know that
please believe me:
it's harder to leave than I ever thought it'd be
yet
helplessly, I'll barrel towards the edge
soaked right through with guilt & a mouthful of
excuses
neither of which are equipped to save me
from the razor sharp rocks that wait below

how can I explain how little I want to plummet over?
is there any way to make you see?
it isn't me, it's a lie
it's my demons shoveling coal into the flames
fueling me, tricking me

in seven short hours
I'll hang there, spinning in mid-air
precariously above my sharp demise
the liquor-laced wind will envelope me
winding colder & colder until
I am a cocoon of ice
a statue, sculpted by my self-prescribed fate
spinning

tomorrow I'll wake back at the station
chugging along to my intended destination
& the only one who'll know I derailed
is me

Let Me Kill You

you whisper sweet everythings in my ear
your intoxicating breath drips down my neck
your strong hand leads me deeper
to the glade, lush & fragrant
you spin me, high & slow
my hair turns to gold in the low molten sun

your lips between my ribs, "let me love you"
I breathe you deeper than my lungs
right into the center of my brain
you become me
I let you love me

I wake to the taste of ash in my mouth
& dead grass that's crumbling beneath me
I crawl & am met with handfuls of brittle weeds
the glade is burning
reduced to nothing but smoldering trees

I'm alone but your whispers find me through the
smoke
"let me—" but I can't hear the rest
the memory is fading, changing,
blurring my sight, blurring my mind
I breathe you in, but I choke on your black soot voice:
"let me kill you"
I become you
& I let you

Manic Intoxication

another day of shimmering freedom
where my only shackle is my skin
my head is full of bubbles & sweetness
only fractionally aware that this could be fleeting

somewhere, far away
there's a darker side of this brilliant silver
a moment along my timeline
that I hope to wholly avoid
but that's for another day, another me

you won't want to hear it, but,
I don't think of you as often &
the thought of you doesn't affect me, as much
I see you in the hands of others,
against the lips of strangers & friends alike
it's not their fault,
you're irresistible
only now, by some miracle, I can't remember why

I will fight to the teeth for
this glimmering light that occupies my mind
for to fall to your manic intoxication
would be every fault, mine

Operation: Overdrive

I am who you say I am
I do what you tell me to
will-power, no more
this is Operation: Overdrive

my thoughts are powered by
greasy black mechanisms
connected to hydraulic limbs,
my joints grind & hiss
this gift you gave:
a cold exoskeleton,
titanium-strong & unrelenting

I do what you tell me to
I beg & crawl
I march & destroy
I'm your soldier
I don't need freedom,
I need your gasoline

over & over I hear your command
until it sounds like my darkest desire
I guzzle your fuel
saturating every cell:
skin, eyes, mind, & soul
the sun abandons me
I'm a human cocktail in the pitch black
burn, Molotov, burn.

lights-out, hard reboot
wake desiccated, desperate, & alone
flick the switch
Operation: Overdrive

Just For a Moment

I forgot you existed

Wake the Fuck Up

it's time
right this goddamned second, it's time
you have to WAKE UP
no more bleary 2pm breakfasts
no more up until dawn
NO. MORE.
your parents are worried sick
your friends feel helpless
your sister hates when you cancel plans
because you're 'sick'
but I bet she knows the truth
eyes bloodshot & sunk to the bone
I don't care if you're scared
I don't care about "maybe tomorrow" or "just one
more"
no, this stops NOW
you're going to have to begin before you're ready
dry up before you drown
'cause no one else is going to catch you
or help you get your feet back on the ground
stop, just stop
no more secrets, no more lies
this ends today
It's time. It's time.
It's time.

A Fool's Forge

I can't believe I missed *this*
is it possible to miss burning alive?
I thought facing the flames was a testament of
strength,
proof that I'd emerged as hardened steel
I wanted to hold my skin to the fire
I wanted to smile through the bubbles & blisters
how foolish I was
it. was. a. trick.
just another damn illusion of the mind to get me here
aren't you tired yet, demons?
tired of chasing me around?
well, congratulations,
your slight of hand worked
can you smell me burning?
are you happy now?

The Whisper

empty everything
your closet, your fridge
your soul, your mind
come void of what you knew to be true
come naked & hollow
you must arrive hungry for something new

this is where you're meant to be
the water,
warm & soothing
will welcome you & make you feel at home
it only appears shallow at first
but do not fear the depths —
the vastness will fill you
& ready you for the wholeness you deserve

float now,
supported & sure,
slip your lips beneath the cascading waterfalls
feel the mist cast off the moss-covered rocks
this place is for you
the knowledge is waiting
can you hear it? that whisper deep within?
if you want it,
you can be brand new

Trust

you're learning to walk through the fire
so that you can guide those in your wake
don't look back
have faith
you are their light
& they're already following

Ruin, Rise

this is a city without walls,
only ruin
venture inside, come now,
explore the rubble
trip over its abandoned foundations
bellow, hands cupped,
into its catacombs
daydream about what once was,
& what will be
there were great battles here, yes,
but despite the aftermath,
they had all been won

Angler Fish

when I was seventeen
David instructed us to sit in a horseshoe
a semi-circle of safe space
one by one we took our turn on the spot of grass
at the opening

we held on to the feel of the cool blades
under our bare feet
& how they irritated the skin of our short-short clad
thighs
we tried to be calm, tried to steady our nerves
though we were anxiously charged,
all of us, during our turn on the stage

my turn was first
affirmations, one at a time rang out from each of my
peers
my job was to sit, listen, & soak them in
to this day there is only one that I still remember,
from Grayson:

"you're placid
like a lake," he said
"so calm & still on the surface,
yet so much more going on beneath"

maybe he got it from a tv show
or a book he'd read
maybe he said it to every girl...

or maybe it was the nicest thing anyone had ever
said

eight years later I am still that placid lake
but the parts below are miles deeper
thirty-six kilometers, to be exact,
like our ocean
there are underwater mountain ranges
& sunken ships
lost souls & broken bones
treasure, if you can find it

atop the soft eddies, I float
sunglasses, a smile, arms starfished wide
but when I'm below, where we often ask,
"is there even a bottom?"
I'm something far more sinister
made of spiny bones & terror teeth
a light, a part of me, the only beacon to be seen
don't be fooled, it doesn't guide the way,
it seeks out prey
as predator seeks out me
because down there, where it's too dark to see
there isn't a witness
to my greed

Surrender

the frost has forsaken us
but in its place, there isn't much green
the snow has said its final farewell
yet the buds are few & far between

the only outcome is prophesied as good
but where is the positivity?
forward we look with forward thinking
yet I've seen how flowers can suddenly freeze

each dawn rises earlier & warmer
but the skies still open with lightning & thunder
a black rain falling, meant to strip us bare
yet we look up, no choice left to us except surrender

Yo-yo

I want fresh cut flowers
& holy ghosts
I want too hot to eat ramen
& chocolate milk

I want this day to last forever
but I can't wait for it to end

X

throw rocks at my body made of glass
I want to know what happens
to all the tiny
pieces

Tell the Fucking Truth Already

the trouble with lies
is their malignancy
each falsity, either spoken aloud
or to yourself
eats you from the inside out
little by little, your cells will die
necrotizing your organs,
your flesh
until you're a shell,
just rags & bones,
& hollowed out eyes

NQTD

never question the decision
not in the late night refrigerator light
not in the hectic, cut you off, daily commute
not in the mid-day moment to yourself
& not at the after-work happy hour, surrounded by
friends saying,
"come on, let's have another"

the beginning will be the worst
you'll be tricked & spun around until you cannot
stand
the false thoughts will sneak in, disguised as truth:
"just one, I'll have just one"
you know it'll never stick, it's game over the second
it hits your lips
"I mean, what's one more? I've already given in"

never question the decision
surrounding you, the lies bombard your conviction:
"chardonnay saves the day!" on your living room
wall &
on your counter, glassware etched with, "It's 9am
somewhere!"
all this poison propaganda

you'll feel left out, you'll feel wrong
they'll laugh & holler
as they put back beer after beer
you'll feel weak, you'll want to scream,
"what the *fuck* is the matter with me?"

but you are every damn thing that's right
you've finally realized what you need:
strength—inside—
the power over the thing that makes their happiness
bleed
never question the decision
not even when you think you're the only one to
succeed

Siege

my mind has walls
I'm not sure who built them
but they're as thick as the concrete ones
in my apartment

I know you're there
you're always there

your hooked teeth &
razor claws
scrape away
scrape scrape scrape
away

I lay with my back against the laminate,
staring at the ceiling
counting down the minutes
until you break through
you always break through

Raw

when did everything get so bright?
the office computers, the fluorescent lights
my eyes are red & leaking
even the sun, warm as it is,
is searing

when did everything get so sharp?
my clothes, my thoughts
my skin is rough & bleeding
even the air, as fresh as it is,
is tearing
me

when did everything get so alarming?
my decisions, my emotions
my heart is raw & aching
even the day, as new as it is,
is daunting

everything, all at once
then nothing, nothing at all
one moment a whirling vortex
& the next, the deepest void
maybe if I close my eyes
& reach out for something, anything
I'll manage, in the whirlwind of it all,
to make it stop

Biological Warfare

a million wings inside my chest
fluttering razor wire,
I can't catch my —
I can't catch my breath

are my lungs expanding? is my heart contracting?
or is my blood pooling right where I rest?
I'm sure my pressure's dropping, or is it spiking,
thanks to the poison I gladly ingest?
pH rock bottom, plasma congealing in my veins
when can I expect
bullet sized clots to head straight for my brain?

White Noise

I'm an attic-buried transistor radio
rusted stuck between two frequencies
where the FM station plays lively, carefree melodies
that remind you of summer skylines

the other is much more frenetic, AM & harrowing,
mumbles & screeches that you can't quite decipher
it isn't summer, it's dead of winter
& the nostalgia it pulls is barren & frigid

the two stations mingle & slice
jarring, then lilting, with sweet moments of soft static
the stimuli is often much more than too much
& the only chance for silence
is to turn me off

Michelle Winder

"hang on to the hope
you will get there, one day at a time
I know it sounds cliché, but you will"

you said this in a moment of sunlight
about fears past & fears
to come

I'll hang on
as cliché as it is
even as my nails break
& my fingers bleed,
with rocks tied to my ankles
& water rising up,
I'll hang on

Hide and Seek

if you quit anything
for long enough
everything you threw, hid, killed
away
catches up to you

Elementary

trying to teach myself
that the blood in my veins
& the dirt on my shoes
are the only coping mechanisms
I need

Coffee

my existence is a french press
my soul is boiling water
when trouble stirs
I compress it down
dark, thick coffee grounds of
chaos trapped below
that yields pure bittersweet stimuli
to get me through the day

Impossible

I've stopped speaking
for my jaw aches from too much clenching
I've stopped writing
for my fingers are embedded in my palms
how do I take five years of pain & fear
that was shoved into the dark, spider-infested
basement of my mind
& feel it?
right here on my couch on a Wednesday evening?

Bloody Mary Midnight

out of visceral habit
my ice tray is always full
I'd rather be caught dead
than without something cold
& bloody in my hand
yet now, dead is how I feel—
caught dead, anyway
you're asleep, alone in our bed
while my head's in the freezer
the ice cubes crash against my glass
loud & guilty
like a punch to my gut,
the red-handed string tightening around my finger
does it wake you?
it's like sorrow in July—
a sentinel of darkness
guarding the slippery slope
to a never forgotten Winter
I'm a virgin now,
you could say
I drink Holy water &
bathe in sacred candle light
oils anoint my palms & feet
I'm clean, I swear I'm clean
yet I'll confess
out of goddamned biblical habit
I'll confess

Pain is a Gift

you must learn your pain
accept it, know it
become it
when it leaves,
the gift remaining is truth
to be your pain
is to be yourself
to free your pain
is to free yourself

Cassandra

dear flamekeeper,
I know you're there—
silent in the shadows of my soul
I choke as you shift your rusted joints
& a decade of dust slides from your shoulders
into my lungs

I can feel your glossy eyes
like a hollow pit—
they bore, unblinking,
at the embers that were once a fire

you've never stopped
never abandoned your post
never once let that flame die
so, I ask you now:
stand, grow tall
stretch & crack your stiffened bones
fill your chest with ancient air
feed this fire
feed me
for tonight we burn this wretched city
to ash
& worship the hidden ground on which
we built it

Ashes

about ten times a day
I want to die
not a physical death,
but a conscious demise
knock me out, bleed me dry,
anything to get me out of my mind

I want to burn alive

Lesson One

start killing the thing that's
killing you

<u>Unmooring</u>

my mind begged to float away
so I severed it at the cord
clouds filled my eyes
until I dreamed of nothing more

Goodnight, City Lights

it's the 1 a.m. desperate reads
of words born from other people's wounds
shapeless inspiration that claws inward
until something stirs
until it's not just their pain anymore,
it's mine
until my throat burns from their screams
until my heart aches from their tears
my wounds are their wounds &
I'm bleeding their blood until I
crack wide open

Beam

I feel nauseas from all the
latent joy unearthing within—
dopamine overload
—and this time, it's the real deal
my miniscule body can't
contain this explosive smile
I'll breathe through the sunshine
& ride the self-induced high

Sat Nam

I have small moments of
absolute clarity
where I can see my life from
start to finish
I understand what anger is &
how to honour it instead of locking it away or
giving it to someone else
I understand why I want what I want
& how to clear a space in my soul for what I
need
but then I breathe too shallow
or turn too quickly
& I forget
everything I thought I knew
is gone & I know absolutely
nothing

Responsible

all around me, it seems,
my friends' hearts are breaking
they're trapped in dark, disgusting places
that they're convinced are the best
that that they deserve
but they deserve the stars
& the planets
& the whole damn galaxy

in my own destructive spiral,
I have found all the answers—
they bite into the tip of my tongue
you always say,
"they have to figure it out for themselves"
"it's not your place"
but what if it is?
what if I'm so broken that I'm the only one
who can prove their worth?
the blood in my mouth is proof enough
there's power in words unsaid

so, what if all it takes is me saying the right thing?
or the wrong thing?
what if it's my stubborn silence in
following some fucked up social norm of,
"they have to reach their breaking point"
that convinces them that it's okay to lay down & die?

Here and Now

remove the smallest
sliver of pain & watch as
the release cracks the dam
& words flow out like an unstoppable flood,
drowning what was
to make space to start again

Irritation

it came as I slept
like a swift invisible bite
& when I woke,
bloodshot despite a restful sleep,
I'd been turned
from maiden to monster,
hungry for anything that
looked my way

Introversion

let me be
holed up inside of myself
safe & stuck between forever silent &
screaming deafeningly
don't play with my hair
don't speak to me like everything is normal
even though it's a sunny Saturday
& we're wasting daylight
you crave outdoor agendas & fresh air
but I need sixteen hours of sleep
let me be, please
don't touch me like I'm yours
even though I am
I haven't told you yet
how sacred my mornings have become
you should *just know* what I need
you should know that if I don't slow down
& breathe deep
& pretend like I'm the only one here,
I'll collapse
like an ill-timed soufflé
removed & fallen
the day ruined on a plate
crumpled & sickly sweet

<u>True North</u>

for the better part of a decade,
loneliness had been my number one excuse
but time has taught me that
loneliness is a blessing,
a powerful agent of change
it's the moment we shift from distraction
to meeting our true selves
our first instinct is to fill the void —
fill it with booze & drugs & sex
& food & followers & selfies
we must fight against this urge
we must greet the loneliness,
sit in the abyss
& welcome ourselves home

<u>Insomnia</u>

here we go
merry-go-round
Fate takes the helm, & spins
g-force pins me to the metal,
I'm helpless
Fate's head tips backward,
her lips curl wide as she brays
into the wind
the colours whir by me, familiar
all these places I've been before
blurred hues of Hell
please don't stop here,
I beg of Fate
please don't stop

Vor í Vaglaskógi

I don't want to write this
this isn't poetry
these are just the only words I have
I've drank a hundred coffees
or, really, it just feels like I have
I want to jump off the 18th floor of my building
the roof
& bury myself in the closet
all at once
I'm crying
& pacing
& faking the lyrics to an Icelandic folk song
or is it pop?
that's where I'm held up at
the decision on what genre this band is
that & how little I want to talk to anyone
yet all I can do is talk talk talk
just *shut up* already
can I just shut up?

Blue Heaven

I took the first plane out of here
when it landed, I didn't come down
I peeled off my shoes, hoping for wings instead
my skin blistered & broke
but I kept leaping off of rocks, climbing trees,
to get closer to the sky
once I had a taste of pure blue,
nothing else would do

Recovery

41 days
23 hours
& 15 minutes
of staring out my north-facing
downtown window,
picking gin bottle shrapnel
out from between my lungs

Baby

I would never have called myself a sensitive soul
to me, sensitive meant 'cry baby'
someone who couldn't handle shit
someone who overreacts

'overreact'
that word is lost to me
aren't we all just having chemical reactions
to other people's chemical reactions?
one big science lab world
the universe tinkering with our beaker brains
until the balance is just right

I am a sensitive person
I'm sensitive to what's real
not to how you react to me reacting to myself
or the world around me

I am a cry baby
an infant, unable to walk alone
but I'm also a mother
who will always carry myself in my arms
gently & unconditionally

I couldn't handle any shit
I wasn't ready
but now I am
because my soul is as sensitive
as the day I was born

Anosmia

I met my future self today
even she knew it
she said, "you're me, only a few years ago"

strangers one minute, sisters the next

we had the same story
the same beginning
her feet, bloody & willing,
had stood exactly where I stand now

she had followed a sense deeper than sight
or smell
to where her heart opened
as mine is opening now
she is a healer
& I, a writer
& we are the same

Sensory Deprivation

1:37am
again
I've just tried to write a poem about our air
conditioner
you love it—
white noise that drowns out the city
& a way to use flannel sheets through the summer
I used to love it too
but I can't take anything these days
that breaks the night time silence

Flashback Friday

waking up late
with no clean underwear
no time for breakfast or
a single second to ready yourself
for the worst day of your life
is not a curse
but a blessing

Fuck You, I'm a Warrior

I beat the cravings
I punched them in their ugly mouths
broke their jaws
kept all their teeth

& when I was done,
I lay down, gory & heaving,
& I asked for another challenge

Groundhoggin'

last night's makeup
only one eyebrow left
messy bun
where messy means knotted beyond rescue
& greasier than the MacDonald's
I had for breakfast the 4th time this week
a pounding 10hr headache
& monsoon waves of nausea
is this all that life has in store for me?

Solo Travel

in eight days time
I'm leaving the North
& heading to the desert
alone, for the first time
& for the first time,
I'll be taking a hike
alone
I dreamt that at the end of the trail
I would die
I know this will come true
& it will be beautiful

Shatter

did I tell you how easy each morning is?
how I feel like one of those Cosmo girls,
braless, white t-shirt, baby-blue panties,
manicured fingers ready
to tousle my perfect bed-head dirty blonde hair
as I fry eggs & sausage for us,
coffee in one hand, a cheeky smile in the other?

have you noticed how short lived that is?
how the accidental drop of a knife
or the tv turned up too loud
breaks me?

can you tell that I walk through noon
with a bomb strapped to my chest,
countdown timer screaming in my ears?
where the only safety is found sunken in ambient
sounds
& absolute stillness?

before this, I feared boredom
what would I do with all my time?
have I told you, boredom no longer exists,
that every moment of my day is a battle for balance?

I'll avoid conversation
I'll avoid the outdoors—
I'm certain that if the sun were to slip behind a cloud
that would be enough for this vest to...
well, if I explode,
you explode, too

Dear Bourbon,

my favourite mug,
filled with you,
shattered last night

my favourite t-shirt,
stained from the accident,
feels like sandpaper as I pack it in my suitcase
"that won't get you very far,"
you point a shaky finger at the broken zipper
it will get me far enough

I want to forget you
you ruin everything I love
& everyone who loves me

a million times I've welcomed you back,
begging on your knees

if I don't go now, I'll never leave

"I won't let you"
you bar the door,
angry bottle of yourself slipping from your hand
it falls, you shatter
dark poison seeps into the floorboards
you strike a match,
"where did you get that?" I say,
like it matters, as flames burn up our eyes
my one last chance reduced to ash
"you have to stay"

Things I Never Told You

I've commandeered the Nike water bottle
(I know, it's yours, I'm sorry)
but mine's still on my side of the bed,
sweating fumes from last night's gin

Numb

you're a shell —
perfectly hollow
a master of self-
abandonment

your sweet bones
discarded lay
fleshless & without
defense

back inside your mind,
horrors await
"come back," they whisper
"we've found new ghosts
for you to meet"

Queen

I am crowned Queen of speaking too soon
at the first sound of silence
I pin a medal to my breast
my foes are gone! beaten! surrendered!
by now
you'd think I'd have learned that
soundless does not mean vanquished
Adrenaline is my only adviser
he thrusts his victory sword above his head
& lets me believe
the fight is my vice
a battle cry for a new war
cuts from my lips
just as my enemies from yesterday
breach my defenses

Cliff's Edge

the higher the climb
the harder the fall
if you're afraid of heights
then don't look down at all
keep your chin up
& your gaze true
what lies below
wasn't meant for you

It Takes a Village

on the high days I'm a Goddess
a lone golden wolf with an iron howl
but the low days tend to hit me quick & fierce,
like a deadly winter gale
my fangs are blown from my jaw
my thick pelt freezes & shatters
& what's left is just a child
without her village

Mind Fuck

I've been down this crooked road before
I've scabs from the splintered concrete
& wounds that refuse to clot,
bloodied by thorns that haunt my dreams

I've ignored the weathered signs,
& the new ones erected by my hand,
"turn back!"
"stop!"
"do not go farther!"
yet...
I know what waits beyond the point of no return
past where the path disappears in a sharp decline

below, the rocky bottom is always the same:
pain, shame, guilt, a haze I can't shake
100 questions without answers & hellfire to pay
endless valleys of self-loathing, emptiness, & anger
10,000 problems shoved under the rug
to be dealt with later

the nothingness will swallow me
I'll beg for death
for some small relief
"let me out! take me back!"
100,000 silent screams

I've been there before
I survived, I still breathe
so what's another go?
what's the worst that can happen to me?

<u>Drinking Again</u>

it's a lot like dropping a vase of flowers
— wholly obliterating
a once well-functioning mechanism disintegrates to
uncontained fluid that spreads without abandon
across the kitchen floor into the forgotten bills on the
unswept tile
& under the fridge to hide

I instantly mourn my clarity
all of my beauty, previously neatly arranged,
is now a mess of disconnected stems
torn petals & tattered leaves
I'm everywhere

my murky water soul
muddled with dust & grime
spreads so thin that it dries in some places
leaving nothing but bits of dirty glass
I wonder:
after I collect myself
will I ever see these parts again?
will I ever, truly, be me?

Brain Fog

my darling,
for you, I try to be the embodiment of honesty
to show you the truth behind my face
though maybe you don't know the gravity,
the context,
the absolute hell that is my smile

every choice to sink into oblivion,
is annihilation
an acid fog that rises from my ashes
to erase me
that's where I try to be honest
I grasp for words that you can grasp
but the mist is so thick that I forget how to speak
without words I'm without explanation
so you tell me it's in my head
"of course it is," I scream,
"nightmares are always on the inside"
but the toxicity is real
it's as real as you & me

British Columbia in Mid-July

thick smoke from the fires in the West
burning trees lead to old homes burning
we choke, in the vastness of the prairies,
on the shadow of others' loss
our eyes stick to apocalyptic skies &
our lungs harbour strangers' sorrow
water, buckets of water is what they need
I'll pray for them & for doomsday rain
while I practice nightly my own version
of drowning

Paper Thin

been giving myself away to anyone who needs it
a sliver of compassion for her
a sliver of 'you talk, I'll listen' for him
all those slivers are from the mirror of me
silver & fractured, held only by cheap glue
that's quickly melting from the heat
of too many late nights
lifting boxes filled with other people's woes

<u>Hawrelak Park Amphitheatre</u>

can they see the cravings
crawling underneath my skin?
my demons, personified, dance
in the blinding light of the setting sun
this was my haven
my dark sanctuary where my sins could fester
I was hidden by the sea of immorality
but like that sun shining across the stage,
my deepest reaches are illuminated
I am exposed for the grotesque being I want to be
let me writhe, let me sweat
let my eyes roll back inside my head
please, take my soul, please
take from me whatever that is left

Venti&Shades

five years running on coffee fumes
to mask a skin that wreaks of rocket fuel
"you got a match?"
you beg me to stop asking that
but I can't shake it
I can't stop shaking
light
me
up

Wendy

I ebb & I flow
I rake my weary water over sand & silt
my underbelly licks rocks that cut
each wave brings new broken shells
each undertow takes them away
like the changing of the tide
these feelings too will fade

WORSHIP (FULL MOON)

my spirit is swinging like a scythe
is it the full moon that pulls my heart-tide
or is it you, again
planting crooked kisses on my shivering feet?

Al-kuhl

I've been having thoughts
—dark ones
the kind that sneak in on your way down the
basement stairs
like a sinister draft that grabs your ankles

the most recent: how our bodies can function
just fine
pumped full of poison, drained of nutrients,
deprived of sleep
—that scares the shit out of me
how can we withhold all goodness & instead
pour chemical after chemical
into us
& still think & walk &
breathe?

something so flammable cannot be human

you've heard we're made of water
but truth is we're made of ghosts
—"spirits"—
bottled, liquid darkness
that haunt the living
so, what evils are we capable of?

PICK YOUR POISON

Acknowledgements

Sobriety takes a village.

I'd like to acknowledge Denise Davis-Taylor for all of
her advice, for giving me a safe space to voice my
struggles, and for turning Remedy Café into a sober
haven for me. I'd like to thank Geoff Casey and Diane
Fluet for continuously checking in on me and calling
me out on my excuses to drink—you helped rewire
my brain. A big thank you to my boyfriend, Liam, for
always supporting me and making sobriety an easier
path to walk. To my parents for making sure I had
whatever I needed. To my favourite sister (wink). To
Maria and Lydia for giving me so much love and
compassion. To my work family for everything that is
US. To Jimmy and his Every Abundance essential oils
that got me through cravings, hard emotions, and
sleepless nights. To Arizona for being the final resting
place of the fake me and for being the birth place of
the real me. To Lael and Andrea for proof reading. To
Colleen for editing. To Michelle, Wendy, and
Cassandra for inspiration. To Maggy and Lael for their
kind words. Thank you to everyone who reached out
to me, gave me feedback, or held my hand, thank
you thank you thank you. Now, before I start
thanking my baristas and root beer slurpees I need to
give the most important shout out of all:

Holly Whitaker saved my life. I found her blog, Hip Sobriety through desperate google searches on how to quit drinking. Reading her blog posts was like reading the inside of own brain. Sobriety finally made sense. She introduced me to Gabby Bernstein and I immediately purchased Gabby's book 'May Cause Miracles' (which it did). I enrolled in Holly's Hip Sobriety School (April-June 2017) which provided me with all the knowledge and love I needed to really succeed in my sobriety.

To my Hip Sobriety School classmates: none of this would have been possible without you. You held me, heard me, loved me, and calmed me. You are everything.

Lastly, I acknowledge you, reader. If you are struggling or know someone who is struggling with addiction please look into Holly and Hip Sobriety. If what she says speaks to you, that is a success. If it doesn't, that is a success too. Any step towards your own wellbeing is a victory. Reach out. Keep reaching out. My inbox is always open.

I love you,
Denise Walker

About the Author

Denise Walker lives along the river valley in downtown Edmonton, AB. Her sober journey began Spring of 2017 and she has since found solace in writing poetry, meditation, and nurturing her fiddle leaf fig tree, 'Figgie'. She works full-time as an Emergency Communications Officer at Ambulance Dispatch. In between shifts she enjoys brewing kombucha, binge-watching TV, and lusting after her next travel destination.

DENISE WALKER